SPEAK CHEROKEE RIGHT NOW

Billie Ruth Walls

NATIVE VOICES
Summertown, Tennessee

Library of Congress Cataloging-in-Publication Data available upon request.

We chose to print this title on paper certified by The Forest Stewardship Council® (FSC®), a global, not-for-profit organization dedicated to the promotion of responsible forest management worldwide.

Native Voices
Book Publishing Company
PO Box 99, Summertown, TN 38483
888-260-8458
bookpubco.com
nativevoicesbooks.com

Printed in the United States of America

ISBN: 978-1-57067-421-1

MIX
Paper from responsible sources
FSC® C000000
FSC www.fsc.org

28 27 26 25 24 23   1 2 3 4 5 6 7 8 9

Dedicated in loving memory of

Leon Gilmore, my brother,

who treasured his Cherokee Heritage.

Panther Clah dah chee

CHEROKEE—YOU CAN SPEAK IT RIGHT NOW.

See the word or sentence you want and say what is written and you are speaking Cherokee. It is all sounded out for you.

If you read and say (oh see yo) you have just said hello. If you say (wah doe) you have said thank you. Just follow your alphabetical list and you will be well understood.

Words ending with ey are said like key.

Words ending with double oo are said like boo.

A

ABOVE gah lay low

ACORN goo lay

AIR oo no lay

AIRPLANE gee you

ALL nee gah duh

ALRIGHT oh sdee

AND ah lay

AND YOU? nee nah?

ANOTHER new dah leh

ANY e new s dey

ANYTHING SHARP POINTED yuh gee

APPLE sunkt

ARE YOU FINE? toe he jew?

ARE YOU HUNGRY? jah you see hahs?

ARE YOU SLEEPY? he tluh skah chuh?

ARM go yah dah

ARRIVE oo lou chuh

ASLEEP gah kllch ha

AT THE RIVER OR CREEK ah may ye

AUNT eh tlah gee

AX gah loo sdee

B

BABY oo sdee

BAD oo yo ee

BALL squah tclay sdee

BANANA quah nen nah

BARREL suh doe nee

BEAN two yah

BEAR yo nah

BEAVER doe yah

BED gah nee

BED COVERS gah nee tluh ah yea stund dee

BEE wah doe ley see

BELT ah dah glos tee

BERRY oo dah tah huh he

BETWEEN ah yay lee

BIG eh quah

BIRD gees gwah

BITE hahs stay geh

BLACK guh nah geh

BLIND dee kay wee

BLOOD gey gah

BLUE sah ko nee geh

BOAT gee you

BOB CAT guh he

BODY oh yea luh

BOOK go whale e

BOTH eh jul lah

BOTTLE goo goo

BOX gah hea sah e

BOYS ah choo jah

BREAD gah due

BREW SOME COFFEE kaw we he gahung gah

BROWN oo woe dee geh

BUCKET suh doe nee

BUFFALO yawn see

BUILD A FIRE hoe yumg gah

BUILDING ah dah neh luh

BULL FROG kah new nah

BULLET gah nee

BUT ah say no

BUTTER go thul nah

BUTTERFLY kah mah mah

BUZZARD sue lee

BY nah uh e

C

CABBAGE jew gah dane nee

CAKE oo gah nah sta

CAME oo lou chuh gee

CAN yea lee qwah

CAN'T clah yea lee

CANDY kahl say gee

CAR deek too len e

CAT way sah

CENTER ah yay tlee

CEREAL sue nah lee ah geh sdee

CHAIR gah ski low

CHEESE oo nud e gah due nuh

CHEROKEE jah leah gey

CHEROKEE LANGUAGE jah leah gey gah woe nee hes dee

CHERRY geh tah yah

CHICKEN gee tah gah

CHIEF oo guh we you he

CHILD ah yo tlee

CHIPS dee gah gwah luh dah

CHURCH jew nee lah wees stey

CLOCK wah gee

CLOTHES due nah woe

CLOTHING dee nah woe

CLOUD oo low gee luh

COFFEE kah we

COME dah ha nah

COME AND EAT ah lee stah edee

COME HERE day hay nah

COOK ah dah stah dee

COOKIES oo gah nah sta

CORN say loo

CORNMEAL gah due ney stah gah yah nee dah

COW wah gah

CRACKERS gah due

CRAWDAD   gess tun

CRY   dee caw no geest

CRY BABY   oo lee yohd dee

CUCUMBERS   gah gah mah

CUNNING   ah dah way he

CUP   ah que gist

D

DAY   e gah

DARK   oo lah see gey

DEAD   oo yo who suh

DEEP   ah s duh gey

DEER   ah we

DID   new duh nah lah

DIPPER   ah que gist

DIRT   gah dah

DIRTY   gah dah hah

DO   nah duh gah

DO NOT   cles dee

DOCTOR   gah nock tee

DOES   nah dun nee

DOG   geet lee

DOLL ah nay low dee

DON'T QUIT nah lah squah de skun

DOOR stew de

DRESS ahsah no

DRINK ah dee tah s dee

DRIVING ah yee lee suh

DROP go hoe sss gaw

DRUM a hoo lee

DRY oh caw youd

DUST kow sss due

E

EAGLE ah woe ha lee

EAR gah lan

EARRINGS ah tdle yah duh dee

EARTH eh low he

EASE wah nah e

EAST jew gah nah wah

EDGE ah s duh e

EGGS jew way gee

EIGHT jah nel

EIGHTEEN neh lah doo

ELDER ah gah yuh lee

ELEPHANT kah mah mah

ELEVEN saw doo

EMPTY oo see whee

ENOUGH doe you duh

ENTIRE nee gah dah

EVEN ee jew lah ha

EVERY nee gah uh e

EYES dah caw nuh

F

FACE oo cah nuh

FAN ah tah no yo

FAR eenah

FAST gah jah nul lah

FATHER eh doe dah

FEATHER oo gee daht lee

FEEBLE oo dah ney lah

FENCE ah so yah

FIFTEEN sgee gah doo

FINE (alright) oh sdee

FINGER gahyah suh guh

FIRE ah tsee luh

FISH a jah dee

FIVE hesk

FLAG gah dat tee

FLOUR e sah

FLOWER oo gey lah skey

FOOD al stah e

FOOT oo lah stan

FOREVER nah go he luh

FORK uh gee

FOUR nuhk

FOURTEEN ne gah doo

FREE oo say goo e

FRESH e jay e

FRIDAY joo nah gee loh sdee

FRIEND oh gee naw lee

FROG ka new new

FRUIT oo dah ton nah

FRY ah shuh tah nuh

FULL hah lee e

G

GARDEN tlo gay see

GATE stew dee

GEESE sah sah

GENTLE oh dahn tee

GET he gey

GET UP tah lay huh gah

GIRL ah gay hugh ah

GIVE ah dah nay dey

GLASS oo luh see dah

GLASSES FOR SEEING deek yah nuh tee

GO oo nah gee sss dee

GO FOR A WALK we nuh juh see yah

GO TO THE BATHROOM doe oh nah juh sdee

GO WASH YOUR HANDS wee tah sul lee

GOD oo nah tlah nuh he

GOLF oo nalah squah low dee

GOOD oss dah

GOT oh gee suh

GRANDFATHER eh do do

GRANDMOTHER jah lee see

GRAPES oo nee tay luh lah dee

GREASE go e

GREAT a quah

GREEN ee jeh yoo sdee

GROUND (like grinding) oh stah uh

GUM ah dlah

GUN gah low gway

H

HAD ah yea huh

HAIR oos tea guh

HALF ah yay tlee

HAMMER gah nuh wah lows sdee

HAND IT TO ME a sku see

HANDS oo woe yan

HAPPY ah ley hah ley s dey

HAVE oh ha

HAY RAKE gah dat tee

HEAD oos col

HEAVEN gah lah no he

HELLO oh see yo

HELP stay lay

HERE ah hah nee

HICKORY NUT so he

HIGH gah luh lah dey

HOG see qwah

HOME jo whey nuh suh

HONEY wah doe lee see

HORSE so guee lee

HOW goo toe e

HOW ARE YOU? toe he juh ney he?

HOW OLD ARE YOU? hah lah e jah day tee yuh dah?

HUGH oo tawn ney

HUMMINGBIRD way lay loo

HUNGRY oo yo see

HURRY new lah

I

I ah yah

I AM AN INDIAN jee yuh wee yah e

I AM FINE oh see gwoo

I AM FINSIHED gess quah dah

I AM GOING dah gay see

I AM GOING TO BED we dah gah nee see nee

I AM HAPPY gah lee eh lee gah

I AM HUNGRY ah gey yo see

I AM PART CHEROKEE jee jah lah gey ah gee guh ha tle

I AM SLEEPY gee cluh skah

I AM TIRED dah geeah way gah

I DON'T KNOW thlah yah gwanh tah

I LOVE YOU gay gay you e

I THINK gay lee ah

I WANT ah gwah do lee

I WANT SOME COFFEE kah we ah gwah do lee

I WANT SOME MONEY ah day lah ah gwah do lee

I WANT SOME WATER ah mah ah gwah do lee

ICE oo nea sdah lee

ILL oh dlung

IN THE WATER AT RIVER OR CREEK ah mah yah

INDIAN ah yuh wee yah

____ IS HIS NAME do doe

IS IT GOING TO RAIN duh gah nah nee chuh

____ IS MY NAME dah wah doe

IT IS COLD doe yah thlah

IT IS HOT oo det ley gah

J

JAIL dee dahs do dee

JESUS gee sah

JUICE oo dah nay nuh

K

KISS oo toe way dawn

KNEE kah nee gan nah

KNIFE hah yast tea

L

LAND gay doe

LAST oh ney

LAUGH oh yeh skuh

LEAD gay nee

LEAVES oo gah low gah

LEG gah nuh skan nee

LET'S GO FISHING e nah sue new gah

LET'S GO HOME gee nah nee gee

LET'S GO TO THE HOUSE kal joe deh wee nee yuh hah

LET'S PLAY BALL e duh lahs gah lah

LET'S SEE EACH OTHER AGAIN doe nah dah go huh e

LET'S SING dee dee no gee

LETTUCE ah ghost ah gets de

LID guh tlud dee

LIQUID gah nah

LIZARD tea yo hah lee

LOCK dah gah see

LOOK hah gah tah

LOUD as s dah yah

LOW a lah dey

M

MAN oh scah yah

MATTRESS ah jas doe

MAY ah nees guh tee

ME ah yah

MEAN scos tee

MEAT hah we yah

MEDICINE nah woe tee

MIDDLE ah yay tlee

MILK oo nud dee

MIRROR ah dah kay dee

MONDAY doe dah wah nuh

MOON muh dah

MOSQUITO doe sah

MOTHER eh gee

MOUNTAIN o dah luh

MOUTH ah hoe lee

MOVE IT he huh nah

MOVIES ah dee yah tuh ski

MUSHROOM we see

MY BROTHER doe stah dah nuh day

MY SISTER uh gee doe

MYSTERY ah day way he

N

NAIL yuh gee

NASTY oh nel tee

NEAR nah uh e

NECKLACE ah yahl dee

NEW e yey

NINE soh nel

NINETEEN soh neh lah doo

NO tlah

NOON e gah

NORTH kew huhn cluh

NOSE ki yah so lee

NOT nahs gey

NUMBERS dee says dee

O

OIL go e

OKAY hoe wah

OLD ah gah yuh ley

ON nah nah

ONE saw gwoo

ONION suh gee

ONLY nah s gey

OPEN ah s due e huh

ORANGE on gee

OTHER nuh dah lay

OUCH ah yo

OUT gah nuh go e

OVER gah woe he loo doe dey

OWL wah who he

P

PAIN a hey s duh

PAINT dee sue we stee

PANTHER clah dah chee

PANTS ah sue low

PAPER go whale e

PATH ah dast tee

PEACE toe he

PEANUT due yah

PEAS too yoon sdee

PENCIL do go wah lo dee

PEOPLE an nee yuh we

PEPPER dee quah yod dee

PHONE dey ley no hah dey

PICKLES gah gah mah

PIE gay les geh

PIEGON woe yey

PILLOW ah yea stow

PIN yuh gee

PINK gey gah gey oo skol luh

PIPE gah nuh nah wah

PLATE tay lee doe

PLAY dee nay low dee

POTATO new nah

POWDER dee quah yod dee

PREACHER ahl gee doe huh sld

PRETTY oo woe do he

PUMPKIN e yah

PURPLE ah duh huhl geh

PUT wah dey yey

Q

QUICK oo lee s dah

QUIET ah yah gah ley

R

RABBIT gees due

RADIO gah woe he s gey

RAIN ah gahs gah

REALLY sld gee

RED gee gah geh

RICE dah lee wee

RING ahl yea sue low

ROAD gah nuh nuh

ROCK nuh yah

ROOM kah nuh sue luh

ROUGH oo yo e

RUNNING ah dah nah wes dee

S

SAD oh yo oo daunt

SALT ah mah

SAND no yah

SATURDAY doe dah gwee da nah

SAW gah nah doe gah

SAY he nay gey

SCISSORS del stow dee

SEA ah mah quo he

SEAT gah dee

SEE ah go wah duh

SEED oo gah tah

SELL gah nah dee nud

SEVEN gwal gwah g

SEVENTEEN gawl gwah doo

SHEEP ah wee

SHOES dee lah sue low

SHORT squh lah

SHUT ah s due dee

SICK oh dlung

SICK PERSON oo dah nee lee

SIT HERE ah hah nee joe dles dee

SIX sue dawl

SIXTEEN dah lah doo

SKUNK dee lee

SKY gah lah low

SLEEP gah tlah e dee

SMALL oo sdee

SMOOTH dah we skah gay

SNAKE e nah dah

SNOW uh gee

SOAP oh tlee

SOFT wah ney gah e

SOMEONE ELSE'S HEART oo dah n doe gey

SOMEONE IS COLD kah nah woe gah

SOUP oo gah mah

SOUTH jew gah no wah

SPIKE yuh gee

SPOON ah dee toe dee

SQUIRREL sah low lee

STAR no gwee see

START ah nee

STICK gahn sdah

STILL toe e

STOMACH oo squot ley

STOP hah lay wes dah

STORE ah dah nah nuh dee

STOVE oh see

STRANGE ah say gey

STRAWBERRY ah nee

STUDENT dee day low quah skee

SUGAR kahl say gee

SUMMER go gay gey

SUN nuh day

SUNDAY doe dahgwah sguh

SUNSHINE ah gah lee

SURE doe you duh

SWEET POTATOES new nah oh nee nuh he dah

SWIM as dah woe s dee

SYRUP wah doe lee see

T

TAKE ah gey s dey

TALK gah woe nee he sdee

TALL e nee gat tee

TASTE new s due

TEA oo gah low gah

TEACHER dee day you huh ski

TEETH day gahn thow duh

TELEVISION ah dee yuh lah tuh ski

TEN sgoh

TERRAPIN dock see

THANK YOU wah doe

THAT nah

THAT'S IT us ski duh

THE he ah

THERE oo nah e

THERE IS ROOM HERE ah hah nee oodlah nuh dah

THEY ARE WALKING ah nah e

THIGH gah gah low

THING e you s dee

THINK ABOUT ah dah nat tah dee sdee

THIS IS he ah

THIS IS MY CHILD he ah ah gway gee

THIS IS MY MOTHER he ah eh gee

THIRTEEN joe gah doo

THIRTY joe sgoh

THREE joe

THUNDER ah yah dah gwah lows gey

THURSDAY nuh gee nay e gah

TIE ah yalds

TILL gey lah

TIME ah lee yee lee suh

TODAY toe he

TOE caw suh duh

TOMATOES tah mah clee

TOMORROW sha nah lee

TOP gah due e

TORNADO oo no lay

TRAIN dee gah jah nul lee

TRIBE ah ney lah s dah luh

TRUE doe you e

TUESDAY tah lee nay ee gah

TURKEY guh nah

TURN ON THE LIGHTS tea juhs tah gah

TWELEVE tahl doo

TWENTY tawl sgoh

TWO tawl

U

UGLY oh nelt tee

UNCLE eh do gee

UP gah lun lah dee tlah

USE gun doe dee

W

WAITING ah gah tea yuh

WALK ah e suh

WALKWAY ah dast tee

WALLS ah juh gah luh duh

WAR dah nah wah

WARM jew gah no wuh

WATCH wah gee

WATER ah mah

WATERMELON guh gey s dey

WAX ah dlah

WAY gah low hes dee

WE eh jul lah

WE ARE WALKING e nah e

WEDNESDAY joe e nay e gah

WELCOME oo lay hah ley s dey

WELL kah

WENT oh whey nuh suh

WEST woo day lee guh

WET gah do leed

WHAT gah doe e

WHAT ARE YOU COOKING? gah doe oo sde huh ne sde?

WHAT ARE YOU DOING? gah doe hah dul nee?

WHAT DID YOU SAY? gah doe gey oss dee?

WHAT IS THIS? do oost he nah?

WHAT IS YOUR NAME? gah doe deh jah joe?

WHAT TIME IS IT? heh lah yuh ah hleel?

WHEEL de gah wah tea

WHEELCHAIR de gah wah tea gah ski low

WHEN he lah e yuh

WHERE gey suh gey

WHERE DO YOU LIVE? hah dluh he nehl?

WHERE IS ___ ? hah tluh?

WHISKEY wee ski

WHITE oo neh gah

WHO caw e go

WHO IS TALKING? kah gah woe nee?

WHY gah doe huh

WIND oo ne ley

WINDOW jo lah nee

WINE gee gah gay

WINTER go lah

WITH nahs squah

WOLF wah hi yah

WOMAN ah gay yah

WON'T cly yea lee

Y

YEAR sue day tea yah dah

YELLOW dah lownee geh

YES uh

YESTERDAY suh he

YET key lah

YOU nee he

YOU ALL COME AGAIN e jeh doe luh e

YOU ALLOWED ME gee ski lee skoal das see

YOU COME AGAIN e heh doe luh e

YOU INVITED ME gee skl lee skoal das see

YOUNG ANIMAL ah gey nah

YOUR HEART oh dahn doe gey

Months of the Year

JANUARY oo no luh tah nuh

FEBRUARY kah gah lee

MARCH ah nuh yee

APRIL kah woe nee

MAY ah nees guh tee

JUNE day hah loo yee

JULY goo yay gwoe nee

AUGUST gah low nee

SEPTEMBER due lees nuh dee

OCTOBER due nee nuh dee

NOVEMEBER nuh dah day gwah

DECEMBER as gey yee

GO	**ah nah gee sss dee**
WITH	**nahs squah**
GOD	**Oo ney tlah nuh he**

Notes

Notes

Notes

Notes

Notes

Notes